Far Out Factoids

✳

Poems by Neil Carpathios

Drawings by Carole Carpathios

FUTURECYCLE PRESS

www.futurecycle.org

Library of Congress Control Number: 2017939670

Published by FutureCycle Press
Athens, Georgia, USA

ISBN 978-1-942371-14-4

For our dear friends, Camille and Paula Sabella

Table of Contents

List of Drawings

Preface

In his 1973 biography of Marilyn Monroe, novelist Norman Mailer refers to what he calls factoids. He defines these strange things as "facts which have no existence before appearing in a magazine or newspaper." He goes on to explain that he created this new linguistic mutation by combining the word "fact" and the ending "-oid" (like a fact). Factoid is also used to mean a small piece of true but somewhat valueless or insignificant information. Often considered spurious and intended to manipulate public reaction, a factoid jolts the brain, stirs speculation, and creates a chain reaction of infinite possibilities to ponder.

The beginning of my personal addiction to these factoids began completely unexpectedly. One day while sitting in the waiting room before my dental appointment, I did what everyone has done: I picked up a magazine and starting skimming. I was not looking for anything in particular, just looking at photos, glancing at the article titles, killing time. Then on one page something caught my eye. There was a photo of a real pig standing in some grass behind a fence, and he had a strange sort of smirk as he gazed at the camera. He also was winking with one eye. It almost appeared as if the pig were enjoying some sort of private secret that no human could ever penetrate. Perhaps the smirk and wink were created through computer graphics, or maybe the photographer actually did catch the pig's image at the precise moment the plump pink animal looked over with its mysterious expression. Whatever the case, I was intrigued enough to read the article, which was about the secret lives of barnyard creatures, and in particular the pig. Although fairly interesting, my attention began to waver, and I really didn't care if my name were called before finishing the article. Then I came to the sentence that would begin a two-year odyssey of factoid research: "The pig's orgasm lasts thirty minutes." I looked back at the photo of that smiling, winking pig, and it all came together. I would be smiling and winking too.

Later that night at home, I sat down at my desk. The strange fact about the pig's sexual endurance came floating back into my mind. I began to wonder about the pig, and why he is able to experience perhaps the ultimate physical pleasure so profoundly. I took out paper and began writing down thoughts, speculations. I ended up with a strange sort of poem. I simply titled it: "A Pig's Orgasm Lasts Thirty Minutes." Then I began to wonder: If this odd fact—this factoid—could spark my imagination, maybe other factoids existed out there that might also fire up some poetic musings. With my trusty computer, surfing the internet, I set out to explore the wonderful world of factoids.

My method was far from scientific. It was purely impressionistic. As I encountered one factoid after another, I wrote down the ones that for some reason struck a chord in me. It was almost like picking berries; I would pluck one factoid, drop it in my mental sack, and leave others on the branch, so to speak. As I sat and meditated on each of the factoids I had collected. I found myself being thrown into surprising corners of my brain. Some factoids launched me into deeply personal memories, both painful and blissful. Some forced me to reexamine my views of the world and the universe. And some just made me laugh. Little by little, I found one poem being born after another. I used the factoid itself as the title for each poem. These were my little factoid babies, my new family of factoid poems.

The notion of a mental trigger to generate writing material is not a new one. Yet, these compelling, bizarre facts seemed to connect me to parts of myself and the world I had not acknowledged before. The factoids were valuable not only as writing prompts, but as reminders to affirm that life is rich with gems that can open up our minds if we only look, only playfully imagine, only entertain the ever-present "what if."

I'll start with my first-born the one that kicked it all off. Oh my beautiful, beautiful pig...

A Pig's Orgasm Lasts Thirty Minutes

Lucky pig.

Did God feel sorry looking down
at all the Christmas hams,
bologna sandwiches,
sausages and hot dogs—
so gave at least one gift
to you to enjoy before slaughter?

If you knew the bloody axe
and butcher's block is where you end,
would you mate all day
milking the mileage of your pleasure wiring,
every half hour oinking in ecstasy?
Would you forget to eat?
Grow bony?
Be set free, no good anymore for anything
but living?

I pass farms on the freeway,
slow to scan for you and yours penned up
or grazing.
I am hoping to see it just once.

Do your eyes roll and roll
like slot machine cherries?
Do you squirm in mud?

Maybe God does have a heart.
Soon you'll be led

to the dark corner of a barn,
trusting the farmer's warm hand,
then hammer-stunned or shot,
hacked into pieces for the butcher
to trim.

The Hummingbird Is the Only Bird that Can Fly Backwards

If he were a man—say, me—
would this power translate to pressing a rewind button
under my shirt?

The rain pours up, the sun rises at night,
flower petals curl and close swallowed by the stem
and the stem shrinks into seed.

The TV says a man jumped off the Empire State Building.
I press my button and voila, the man's eyeballs fly
back into his reassembled skull,

his blood flows back into his body on cement,
his teeth like tiny white moths float back to their nest
in his mouth, and his arms and legs reassemble

as he rises to the ledge then moves back through
whatever pain brought him to this spot.
I watch his wife come back, unpack the suitcase,

unwrite the Dear John letter—*I realize now
I never really loved you* sucked back into the pen.
I move him back to the day he and his wife first

made love, their faces twisting, every muscle tense
at the moment of release, *Oh god Oh god* like birds
pulled back into their mouths. I go further still

to their first kiss, to the moment they first glimpse
each other in a room. I watch his bald spot darken,
his pot belly flatten. I watch him turn into the boy

with the black eye and crooked ball cap, the toddler
gumming a slice of bread. Then slime-covered,
he slides back into his mother's womb,

her legs close up, her belly rises again. I look hard
at his squinched-up face and see he is eager
and hungry—like any thing about to be born—

for the life that is his, however short or long,
his tiny head thumping the wet inner walls,
his pearl-sized fingers searching for a switch.

Goldfish Have a Memory Span of Three Seconds

He glides in and out
of a hollow blue castle
eyeing flaky dust
my god-like hand dropped
still floating on the surface.

Am I really hungry?
Or did I just eat?

I can hear him thinking.

Is he angry bumping his head
every third second
against the invisible
wall of time
the way I've walked
into sliding glass doors
after too many martinis?

How did I get here?
Where is my mother?
Was I ever kissed?

Or is he grateful
to escape
the baggage I carry—

the son hugging his G.I. Joe with grape jelly stains
on the plastic cheek, the daughter
looking down at her feet
as the man tries to explain

divorce, saying they'll have two houses
now, two Christmases, two birthdays,
double the toys,
like a used car salesman trying too hard?

He is the only pet
I've had with two
names I alternate:

Today is Monday—he's Lucky.
Tomorrow, Tuesday—he's Cursed.

He looks out from his glass prison;
I look at the sky.

What does he think
circling the toy diver
whose oxygen tank never empties,
who swims forever
suspended in the same spot
by the castle?

The Female Mite Creates Her Own Husband From Scratch

She lays eggs that hatch into adult males
without needing to be fertilized

then chooses one to copulate with
which dies quickly after; thus never

has to worry about human things
like cellulite or sagging boobs or boobs

too small, or if she's pretty enough;
never has to wonder if a man will one day

ogle other women, beat the children;
never has to be the little girl

who pictures her Prince Charming
but a parade of losers breaks her heart

over and over, so finally she settles
on one who can't measure up,

has to dream her perfect mate
behind eyelids every night, the one

she creates like the mite,
and her husband wonders why

she talks sexy in her sleep,
cradles the pillow—

and they both wake, stare, puzzled,
at the tear-soaked sheets.

The Female Ferret Will Die If She Goes into Heat and Cannot Find a Mate

Unlike the female woman
who touches herself in the shower fantasizing
about the UPS delivery man with rolled up sleeves
tattooed biceps, the female woman who rubs her crotch
against the washing machine as it hums
making the folding of towels for once not boring,
the female woman who unbeknownst to everyone around her
sitting in the coffee shop feels a tickle then a trickle
between her legs reading the novel becoming for an instant
the main character seduced in a restaurant
by the man reaching his hand under the table
sliding his fingers under her dress,
the female woman who surfs singles on the Net,
who wears makeup and jewelry exercising at the gym,
who drops by the sports bar on Sundays,
who tells everyone she doesn't need a man
she is in charge of her destiny and happiness,
the female woman who has learned the secrets of survival
unlike the poor ferret a slave at the mercy of its own smoldering desires.

Approximately 68% of Everything Said by a Person Is Not True

Is what she says in bed to me a lie—

or something she has already said,
in another bed, to somebody else?

Though meant, perhaps, to draw us closer,

it sets me adrift in thought instead—
to somebody in another bed,

myself in the dark beside her warm flesh

saying what I thought she wanted to hear.
Though meant to draw her closer, not adrift,

it made her shiver: to know that I knew

by heart what the heart craves. Like now,
me with a sudden chill hearing what I think I hear.

Someone Gets Divorced Every 10-15 Seconds

I read this in a coffee shop
in a *Psychology Today* article
titled, "The Death of Love"

while a man and woman sit
at the next table
not talking.

They look everywhere
but into each other's eyes.
The woman sips her cappuccino,

keeps checking her watch;
the man never once looks up
from his newspaper.

I see him wiping off the saliva
of her morning kiss. I see her
discussing the grocery list

in the middle of intercourse.
Does she notice the smell
of his sneakers and remember

guys with stronger arms?
Does he wish she would lose
twenty pounds? I see the beast

lying there with flies above
its rotting flesh. The man
and woman ignore it

between them spread across
the table. They put their coffee
cups on its belly, their bagels

on its forehead. They lug it
wherever they go.
They have grown used to

the weight. They would laugh,
call me crazy
if I told them, according to the article,

they killed it.

1 in 5 Children Who Watch Cartoons Believe the False Reality Presented

Saturday mornings since the divorce
it's our ritual. Worth the risk.

My son never asks how the coyote can scoot off the cliff,
his scrawny body running in place,

not knowing nothing's beneath him,
only falling after he looks down;

or how after he falls miles and miles
to the canyon floor, making a small puff of dust,

he can return in the next frame,
his flattened body springing back to shape.

He never asks how Bugs Bunny can draw a door on a rock
only Bugs can pass through, anyone else

who tries crashes into the rock;
or how dynamite can blow up in Tazmanian Devil's belly

after swallowing what he thought was a rabbit,
experiencing what looks like a violent belch,

his body expanding, contracting, his eyes bugging,
a second later madder than ever,

searching out the real rabbit. He's never wondered
why no one's getting therapy,

why no one suffers grief, illness,
why no one dies.

I suppose I should worry.
But when Elmer Fudd,

about to propose to his ugly bride, on one knee,
says "I'll love you forever,"

my son says "Daddy let's watch something else,
this isn't real."

Women Remember Their First Kiss
More Than Men Do

I will remind my son of his.
Maybe as we talk like man-friends
when I buy him his first beer.
Like a hypnotist I'll say, Let me take you
back to 2005, you're eleven
and playing a video game called *Bully.*
With buttons you control
a kid on a high school campus.
Press one button, he spits in his teacher's face.
Press another, he throws a stink bomb
into the lav. Press this one,
he spray-paints graffiti on the school's brick wall.
Press that one, he sets off the fire alarm.

It's fun being bad with a virtual self.
You strut up to a girl on the screen,
offer to carry her books. She agrees
and you walk down a path to a field
of daisies. You press a button that makes
you bend over, pick one for her.
She takes it then moves close to your face,
kisses you on the mouth.
I will tell him how his first kiss was with
a computer-generated girl in a plaid skirt.
How for a half-hour he forgot about spitballs,
cutting class, getting into fights. How he
seemed to be practicing for the real thing,
studying how the kid cupped the girl's chin
in his palm, how the girl tilted her head
to allow noses to fit.

I will ask him if he remembers a tingle
below the skin that like a drug pinned him
to that spot as he kept pressing a replay
button again and again, then another
that froze the two faces lip-locked.

Grasshoppers Have as Many as 400 Distinct
Songs to Woo a Mate

They are the poets who during their human lives
made a deal with the devil,
agreed to one day be trapped inside
the little green bodies

in exchange for even greater genius.

They are Shakespeare, Dante,
Shelly, Keats,
Dickinson, Whitman, Neruda.
And the others.

They died, were reborn.
All they can do is sing, sing, sing
their hearts out.

I see one in the grass just sitting.
I study his tiny face.

Byron? I whisper.
Ezra? Tu Fu? Sappho?

He looks as if he's trying so hard to remember.

There Are More Living Organisms on the Skin of a Single Human Being Than There Are Human Beings on the Surface of the Earth

I knew I felt whole villages on my arm.

That itch was an earthquake killing thousands.
And when I scratched,
how many more did I wipe out:
buildings, bodies, landscapes
mangled under my nail?

To think, right now, some creature on my neck or back
picks his nose while another cuts the lawn
while another jumps off a skyscraper while another
makes love while another sings to himself in a shower.

Each time we kiss,
how many do we kill?
I wash my hands and look hard
at the water in the sink.
I strain to hear microscopic screams.

Sometimes I swear an orgy is happening
between my knee and thigh.

Am I their god?
Do they pray to me on Sundays
in churches in my bellybutton?

Do they know that I know they are there?
Do they try to communicate,
setting small fires
which is when I feel a twitch?

The First Leap Second Was Recorded on June 30, 1972, and Now Occurs Once Every Two Years

It happens when a moment gets stubborn.
The moment watches the moments before it step to the cliff and
    jump off.
The moment wants to live forever.
He reaches the front of the line, digs in his heels, refuses to jump.
The moment behind pushes him over the edge,
but the stubborn moment clings to a tree growing out from rocks.
God says, *enough's enough.* He works free each tiny finger
from around the branch; the moment falls like all the others to
    its death.
God hopes no one notices the slight bulge in time
the stubborn moment's refusal creates.

In a classroom a teenager whose stomach growls looks up at the clock,
    rubs his eyes.

In a waiting room, everyone pretends to read,
            embarrassed to ask if anyone notices the air feels soupy.

Two lovers say goodbye forever.
        The words float above them
                as if waiting to be sucked back into their mouths.

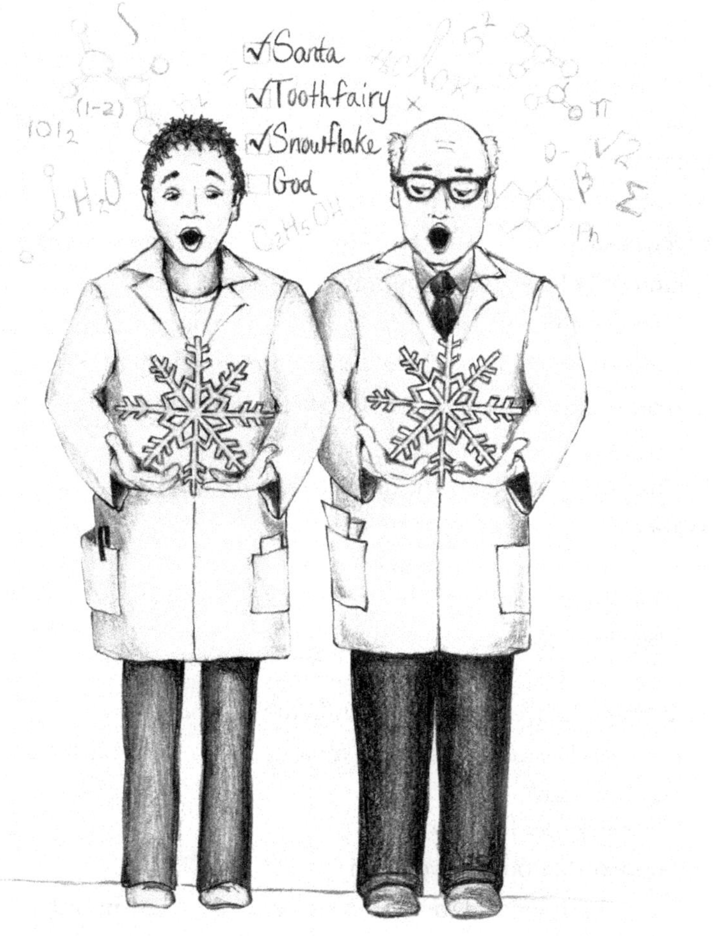
√Santa
√Toothfairy
√Snowflake
God
H2O
(1-2)
C2H5OH

No Two Snowflakes Are Alike Is a Myth;
Some Snowflakes Are Exactly Alike

Well thank you, Harvard scientists
who did the study
and published the results
in a science journal,
which of course was picked up
by every paper in the country
for us sitting down to breakfast
to read this perfect
lazy Sunday morning in December.

I picture the aha moment
when finally two flakes matched,
all the PhDs in white lab coats
giddy, hugging, drenching
each other with champagne
like a locker room after the Super Bowl.

They check *snowflakes* off their list,
just below *Santa* and *Tooth Fairy*,
and just before *God*.

I look out the window
as flakes drift, settling on
other flakes already grounded.

Maybe they're God's crystal tears
as He watches a sad movie
in which mortals choose
knowledge over beauty.

For example,
the thing inside the shells of their bodies
like a far-off muffled ocean
barely audible
in each other's presence—
how they spoil it, He thinks.
By explaining. By settling on a word like
love or *desire* or *longing*.
Or by insisting it's not there.

Maybe God doesn't cry at all
but gets fed up,
turns the channel,
shakes the snow globe
on His mantel.

A Whale's Penis Is Called a Dork

And all those years we never knew,
christening each other in high school halls
when someone dropped
his books
or slipped down stairs
or couldn't open his locker.

It sounded right,
like a strange, nubby mutant troll
or the goofy cartoon stork
who delivered babies to the wrong mothers.

Maybe the first kid to use it
found it while being forced
to read *Moby Dick*,
excited to have gained
at least one small thing
from the avalanche of whale terminology
page after page.

I picture him writing it
on his hand,
then on the bus
spitting it at the kid he couldn't stand
or later at his little brother
screaming it through the bathroom door.
Soon it catches on,
right up there with
doofus, butthole, and *retard.*

Sometimes you still hear it
on playgrounds,

in classrooms,
when one kid needs
the perfect name
and in the millisecond it takes
to flip through the mental rolodex
of put-downs,
he finds it,
yells it out

not knowing he is really complimenting
his buddy's manhood
since it weighs hundreds of pounds
and can reach the length of a small SUV.

The Tiny Dot Over the "i" Is Called the Tittle

Picture the professor who named it.
Middle-aged, balding,
uses a monocle
not out of necessity
but for style.

He lives in New Hampshire
with his three cats.
He sips Earl Gray tea
and hunches over heavy books.
Bushy eyebrows,
nostril hair spiking,
bow tie.

He has a plaque on the wall
verifying he is the one.
He brags on first dates
and lists it in bold print
on his resume.

The name is sexy, he thinks.
Makes a person picture nipples.
Nipples gently twisted, pinched.
Maybe even nibbled.

At parties he works it into every conversation,
sips his sherry explaining how the name
came like divine inspiration.

He sleeps well,
like all great men who know

they have added something important
to the world.

Neil Armstrong. Einstein. Eli Whitney. Beethoven.

The man who made the "i" the most erotic of letters.

Each Year, More People Are Killed by Teddy Bears than by Grizzly Bears

Most Obvious:

Baby left in crib.
Parents turn out lights, leave the room.
Cuddly (jealous) toy opens one eye,
sees the coast is clear,
pounces on baby's face, smothering.
Now the parents are mine, teddy bear thinks.

Less Obvious:

Drunk hubby comes home to nagging wife.
Argument ensues.
Hubby grabs nearest weapon—
Junior's teddy on the sofa.
Hubby pummels wife, then threatens:
"One more word out of your mouth,
just one more word..." and of course
there's one more word.
Hubby uses teddy to gag wife.
Victim found next day on floor,
teddy bear sprouting from mouth.

Least Obvious:

Horny grandpa left alone in house.
Watches infomercial about new Wonder Bra.
Wanders room to room searching.
Nothing even close. But wait:
baby granddaughter's teddy bear.
Sort of exotic, fuzzy, dark.

Hard plastic O of the mouth.
Right in the middle, parents walk in.
Grandpa seizuring, shocked, has heart attack.
Teddy bear needs therapy,
is thrown in garbage.

Donald Duck Comics Were Banned in Finland Because Donald Doesn't Wear Pants

Meanwhile,
in other headlines:

Ten Year Old Girl Raped By Fifteen Men
In Atlanta Three Days Straight.

Child Soldiers Used As Suicide Bombs In Iraq,

Gunman Kills Twenty On Elementary School Playground.

But let's consider Donald.

Hats-off to the Fins.
Incredible that he got below our radar.

How many citizens find themselves aroused,
inexplicably, at parks or zoos,
near lakes and ponds,
by ducks waddling their sexy rumps?

What damage was done by unsuspecting parents
turning on *Loony Tunes* Saturday morning cartoons?

In how many locked bathrooms do horny teens,
confused, hole-up with *National Geographics*—
the "Ducks of the World" issue?

At least in Finland the world is better,
despite picketers, letters
to the editor demanding Donald's return—

but not with graphically inserted pants
to cover his white feathered ass, no;
just the way he obviously wanted
to go through life,
nonconformist,
wearing a silly shirt and hat,
nothing below the belt.

Over 10,000 Birds a Year Die from Smashing Into Windows

They go to a special corner of heaven,
having given their lives.

I picture them being greeted,
handed an umbrella drink,
hors d'oeuvres,
given a kiss on the cheek.

They enlisted,
volunteered for the job
back inside the egg;
they wanted to be heroic.
Or somewhere in there,
under the shell,
did they sign their names
on the dotted line,
tricked by some smooth-talking
recruiter-god?

Was their mission
to try to enter places humans
live big important lives?

Bones and beak and feathers
explode, stopping your heart.
You see the smudge on glass,
think: *how sad, how sad,
it didn't have to be,*

as a newsman on TV behind you
announces the new tally
of how many U.S. troops,
young heroes,
sons, daughters,
have died.

Of All Creatures, Elephants Are Most Like Humans in Reaction to Their Dead

They walk up to a carcass
in tight groups,
hold out their ears
like satellite dishes,
become tense.
They take turns touching the remains
with trunk and feet,
then smell the dirt and hover
swaying back and forth
drunk from something welling up
they can't name.
They each tear off a chunk,
carry it for miles
to drop in some secret spot.
Do they not want us
who might make jewelry of the tusk
and furniture of the giant bones
to find their brother?
Or do they scatter what is left
to hide the evidence,
maybe from themselves?

I remember.
To the open casket
we each skulked,
looked down at my father's face.
Some whispered words,
some stroked his frozen hair,
some made the sign of the cross,
some kissed their fingertips then touched
them to his waxy lips.

An hour later,
we loosened our ties.
We ate and drank and even laughed,
a kind of scattering,
then went home,
crawled into bed,
turned on the TV
watching for tomorrow's weather.

A Thirsty, Dying Plant Will Cry Out for Help, Making a High-Pitched Sound Too High for Us to Hear

Does the cat hear, with its thirty-two muscles in each ear?
Does the ant, circling the fallen cookie crumb on the kitchen floor?
Does the fly, sitting on the counter?
Surely the other plants listen,
feeling helpless,
imprisoned in pots.

I remember holding my father's hand
in the hospital room near the end
in his coma,

closing my eyes,
wondering.

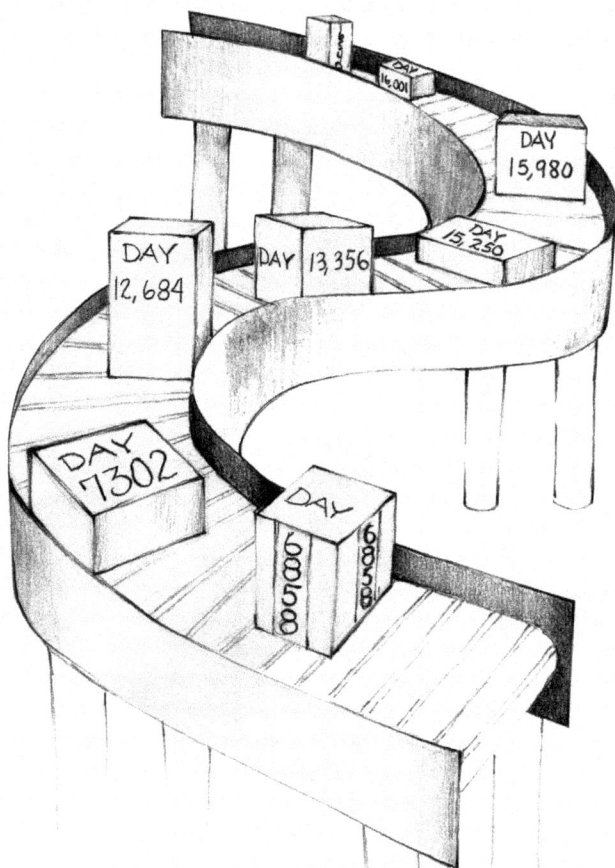

83% of People Believe in a Perfect Day

—for Lester

When my friend found out
he didn't have long to live,
he said he never stomped grapes with his bare feet,
never swam naked in a river,
never spent an entire night staring up at stars,
never made love with a woman who couldn't speak English.

He got philosophical.

We measure our lives by paychecks,
marriages, vacations, deaths.
We live frame to frame like a giant cartoon.
We fill our pockets, like children, with dirt and stones.

He went on.

We like to see the days pass,
though we don't want to reach our last
for a long time. We see ourselves
on a conveyor belt.

Meanwhile,

birds sing outside our window.
Every hour our daughter, our son grows taller—
closer to the moment when we will not have to bend for a kiss,

when we will not get a kiss.

We study a day, say: No, this isn't the one I've been looking for.
We wait for the next and the next when
we are convinced our lives will start for real.

Oak Trees Do Not Have Acorns Until They Are Fifty Years Old or Older

Which is reassuring,
if the acorn is not a cancerous growth,
or an arthritic nub,

if you choose to see it
as a gold nugget
sprouting only after days
and nights of wind and snow
and maybe even the gash
of lovers' initials in the oak's thick skin,

if you make it a symbol of, say, wisdom
that complexifies, the way
certain wines mesmerize
the tongue
only after sitting in dank cellars
nearly forgotten,

if you believe they are
the oak's gift to the world,
a small offering,
a way of saying thank you
to creation for the chance
to stand beside others,
to feel cool grass,
to drink rain,
to gleam in moonlight.

Da Vinci Spent Twelve Years Painting Mona Lisa's Lips

To get a thing right, just right,
and what could be more important
than a woman's mouth?

Did they swell, darken,
shrink, grin
each time he stood

before the canvas trying
to decide
the perfect frozen state,

the one moment apart
from the rest
where beauty intersects

with need, where the slight
curve pinches at the corners
then straightens again

as if about
to speak, perhaps,
his name or

flex the dark ridged flesh
at the pre-birth millisecond
of a kiss?

Was it like trying
to capture the rose's petals
quivering so slowly

no human eye can see,
to witness blooming itself
in blur of process,

to pinpoint
the final pregnant dot
of time before birthing

what we call a blossom?
Did he give up, finally
thinking enough's enough,

finishing at last
to see her as she'd be
forever? Did he think

art is no ending,
only willful saying of
goodbye?

Did he step back
in his body,
scanning the mouth,

wondering if he
got it right, glad
to have started and stopped

so many mornings
after sleepless nights
seeing the lips

through the dark
like a permanent kiss
on the ceiling?

A One-Minute Kiss Burns Twenty-Six Calories

At last, the perfect diet.

No need for recipes, charts, motivational tapes.

They should have kissing spas.
For a fee,
beautiful attendants will let you kiss them for hours.

A diet to shed pounds and ignite passions.

Picture all the happy fat people lining up,
forking out dough.

Maybe you'll steal this idea,
write *The Kissing Diet* book,
star in your own infomercials,
make a million dollars.

You have my permission.

And don't worry;
there are plenty of lonely people
who don't have someone to kiss for free.

Men Are Six Times More Likely to Be Struck by Lightning Than Women

Is it because men are, generally, taller?
Or do we have more fillings,
mouths full of metal?
Or are we just more reckless and stupid?

It rains, a rumbling
in the clouds
as I sit on my stoop pondering—

and yes,
my neighbor, Bob, to my left
still pushes his mower,
ignoring the first flashes
like veins in God's forehead,

and my other neighbor, Jim,
starts out for a jog,
i-pod ear-pods piping, I imagine,
ACDC into his head.

Does God like to punish us
for thinking we run the show
while our women scrub the floor,
stir the stew,
fret over hip size
and ignore our chest-thumping machismo?

Each time another bolt french-fries a golfer
on some hill

I imagine God drawing a line
on a chalkboard,
keeping score,
thinking to Himself,
nice shot.

A Shrimp's Heart Is in Its Head

Which must make the shrimp uniquely rational
during throes of passion unlike most beings,
unlike us; the way we stripped in the kitchen
unable to wait even the few seconds it takes
to walk to the bedroom, and on a chair
next to half-eaten tacos, glasses stained
with Hawaiian Punch you rode me, your hand
over my mouth then mine over yours to stifle
the cum-cries, our kids in the other room
watching *Shrek* hopefully loud enough
with his silly accent to drown out *thump, thump, creak*
of wooden legs on linoleum; the way we risked
being caught, having to explain God-knows-what, God-knows-how,
an x-rated movie playing out instead of dishes
being responsibly washed—the way we pictured our parents—
one handing a bowl to the other to wipe,
fully clothed, talking about the weather.
No shrimp ever was so
reckless, happy, horny I'm thinking as I sit
in a crowded room with smiling people, missing you,
and dip the cold creature in spicy red sauce
then bite, so content none of them has any idea whatsoever
when I say that that's best shrimp I ever tasted.

Eskimos Have at Least 236 Words for Snow, and Some Invent a New Word Every Few Years

I tell her this when she asks why I don't say *I love you* more.
I say, the sparrow sits on the branches in my heart
choosing not to sing in order to learn its song right.
I say, *My bones are candles you light with your touch.*
I say, *The stars are your eyes, the wind is your hair.*
Your body smiles like water. I tell her the same words
over and over is like settling for the sidewalk
winding through the foreign city everybody walks
instead of the dirt path, cobblestone alleys, flattened
sugarcane barely walkable by the ocean.
We follow someone else's idea
instead of learning the wilderness
of beauty, getting lost happily without maps.
We sing too soon the same song.
Eskimos know words are not the destination
but a way of moving toward a thing
to get closer to it. I say,
if she were behind a window, me on the other side,
I'd be an insane bird smashing over and over
against glass.
If she were a melon, I'd be ants on the melon.
If she were the ocean, I'd be the shore.
I tell her the sparrow is working hard
even though it appears to be just sitting.

Crocodiles Swallow Stones to Help Them Dive Deeper

I close my eyes and see my teenage son surprising me,
letting me hold his hand as we cross the busy street downtown.
I play the recording I keep in a vault behind my ribs
of my daughter laughing so hard she can't breathe
that time she fell in a pile of leaves.
I gulp and hold my breath. I open the ribcage like a door.
I swim inside and push the lungs to more easily get to
my father's face, eyes closed never to open again
on the hospital bed, to my mother after too long missing
finding her in the lady's room weeping.
I move the liver, lift the spleen. I find there curled up
the light bulb burning out over my head
my first Christmas alone after the divorce,
the phone not ringing in the dark. I touch the memory;
it twitches. I stare a long time at their Disney toothbrushes
in plastic mugs near the sink. At his ball cap on the bedpost.
Her crayons. Yes, I slide deeper through muck
till I bump against the sitting on my roof,
listening to the crickets; waiting and waiting
for the moon like God's face, telling myself
if it joins me I'm forgiven if not more penance.
I swim a little further, behind the stomach, around the spine,
near the heart. I come up for air. Somewhere
in its reptilian brain the crocodile knows the surface
is sufficient. It can find plenty to eat there, it can
survive. Stones taste gritty, mossy, dirty. Sometimes bitter.
And yet. I think of Jonathan's impish smile.
I think of Ali's hair.

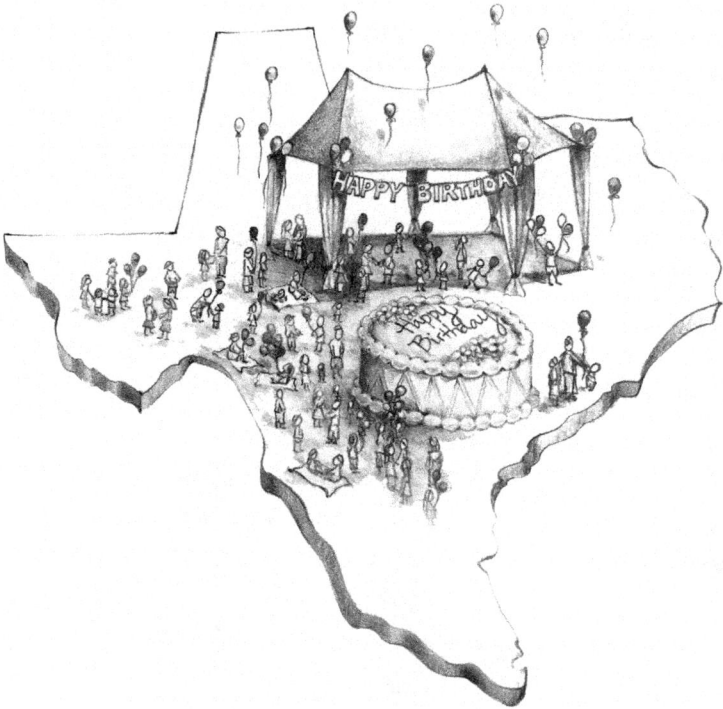

You Share Your Birthday with 9 Million Others in the World

Let's have one big party,
rent the state of Texas for the day.
Pitch a giant tent,
bake a giant cake,
barbecue a few thousand cows.

Let's get to know each other at last,
share photos of family,
tell our stories of pain and bliss,
swap phone numbers,
promise to stay in touch.

We'll welcome new members,
make a career of honoring our birthday kin.
And by the time another year has passed
we'll start over, bake another cake, slaughter more cows,
chew the fat about anything but funeral plans.

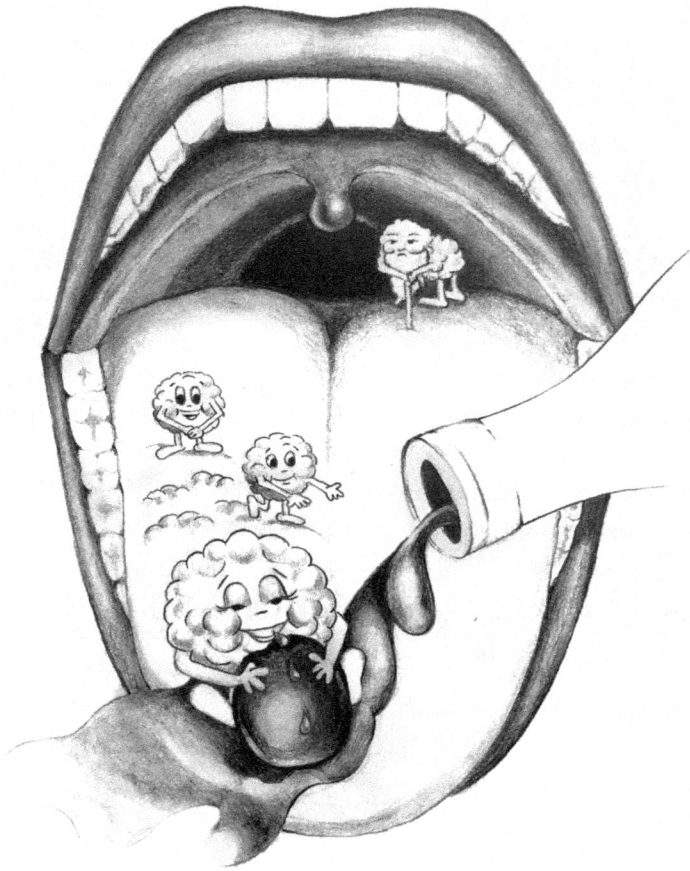

The Lifespan of a Taste Bud Is 10 Days

Ripe grapes,
sourdough bread, feta cheese.
Italian ice, breadsticks dipped
in marinara, almonds.
Lemons, dark coffee, pinot noir.
Cinnamon toast, blueberry, avocado, honey...

                *

Day ten at the end,
do you look back
at what defined you?

In a starving mouth
are you glad to go?

                *

What knowledge you brought,
teaching me item by item —

oh, sweet metaphor of gratitude.

                *

This place.

Like no other.

Acknowledgments

Grateful acknowledgment is made to the following publications in which these poems first appeared, sometimes in slightly altered form:

5 AM: "Goldfish Have a Memory Span of Three Seconds"
Section 8 Magazine: "A Whale's Penis Is Called a Dork,"
    "No Two Snowflakes Are Alike Is a Myth: Some Snowflakes
    Are Exactly Alike"
Slant: "Men Are Six Times More Likely to Be Struck by Lightning
    Than Women"
Solo Flyer: "A Pig's Orgasm Lasts Thirty Minutes," "The Tiny Dot
    Over the 'i' Is Called the Tittle," "A One-Minute Kiss Burns
    Twenty-Six Calories"
Talking River Review: "A Shrimp's Heart Is in Its Head"
The Chaffin Journal: "The Hummingbird Is the Only Bird that
    Can Fly Backwards"

"Goldfish Have a Memory Span of Three Seconds," "The Hummingbird Is the Only Bird that Can Fly Backwards," "Men Are Six Times More Likely to Be Struck by Lightning Than Women," and "Crocodiles Swallow Stones to Help Them Dive Deeper" all previously appeared in *Beyond the Bones* (FutureCycle Press).

"The Female Ferret Will Die if She Goes into Heat and Cannot Find a Mate" and "A Shrimp's Heart Is in Its Head" previously appeared in *Playground of Flesh* (Main Street Rag Publishing Company).

Cover design and drawings by Carole Carpathios; interior book design by Diane Kistner; Caudex text and titling

About FutureCycle Press

FutureCycle Press is dedicated to publishing lasting English-language poetry books, chapbooks, and anthologies in both print-on-demand and Kindle ebook formats. Founded in 2007 by long-time independent editor/publishers and partners Diane Kistner and Robert S. King, the press incorporated as a nonprofit in 2012. A number of our editors are distinguished poets and writers in their own right, and we have been actively involved in the small press movement going back to the early seventies.

The FutureCycle Poetry Book Prize and honorarium is awarded annually for the best full-length volume of poetry we publish in a calendar year. Introduced in 2013, our Good Works projects are anthologies devoted to issues of universal significance, with all proceeds donated to a related worthy cause. Our Selected Poems series highlights contemporary poets with a substantial body of work to their credit; with this series we strive to resurrect work that has had limited distribution and is now out of print.

We are dedicated to giving all of the authors we publish the care their work deserves, making our catalog of titles the most diverse and distinguished it can be, and paying forward any earnings to fund more great books.

We've learned a few things about independent publishing over the years. We've also evolved a unique, resilient publishing model that allows us to focus mainly on vetting and preserving for posterity poetry collections of exceptional quality without becoming overwhelmed with bookkeeping and mailing, fundraising activities, or taxing editorial and production "bubbles." To find out more about what we are doing, come see us at www.futurecycle.org.

The FutureCycle Poetry Book Prize

All full-length volumes of poetry published by FutureCycle Press in a given calendar year are considered for the annual FutureCycle Poetry Book Prize. This allows us to consider each submission on its own merits, outside of the context of a contest. Too, the judges see the finished book, which will have benefitted from the beautiful book design and strong editorial gloss we are famous for.

The book ranked the best in judging is announced as the prize-winner in the subsequent year. There is no fixed monetary award; instead, the winning poet receives an honorarium of 20% of the total net royalties from all poetry books and chapbooks the press sold online in the year the winning book was published. The winner is also accorded the honor of being on the panel of judges for the next year's competition; all judges receive copies of all contending books to keep for their personal library.

www.ingramcontent.com/pod-product-compliance
Lightning Source LLC
Chambersburg PA
CBHW070011100426
42741CB00012B/3191